D1256354

The Super Short, Amazing Story of David and Goliath

Written by Scott and Chrysti Burroughs; Illustrated by Scott Burroughs

Dedicated to our sons,
Maximus and Titus

KREGEL
Kidzone

Many thanks to
our friends and family
for their love and support!

Long ago on Judah's hills there echoed a terrible rattle
of swords and spears as two armies faced off for terrific battle.

On one hill stood the Philistines, who were nasty and smelly and mean.
On the other, God's friends, the Israelites, with a battle line in between.

The Philistine's secret weapon was Goliath, the champ of their tribe.
He stood a colossal nine feet tall, his face too scary to describe.

His breath was the very baddest of bad. He smelled the worst in the crowd.
and as he swung his giant sword he shouted the loudest of loud.

4

"Your god is weak and foolish! You're just chickens filled with fear!"
For forty days Goliath yelled and waved his giant spear.

"Send your best man to fight with me—if he wins then we'll serve you!
But if I crush him—and I will!—serving us is what you'll do!"

Now David was a young shepherd, who loved God and always did good.
So when his brothers went off to war, he wanted to help where he could.

He loaded up food for Israel's troops to keep them big and strong,
but when he arrived he knew right away that something was terribly wrong.

Then David ran to the battle line to see what was going on, and there he saw Goliath, who had been shouting at them since dawn.

Israel's troops were ready to run for they had heard enough. But David thought, "Why are they scared? He's not so big and tough!"

Meanwhile, King Saul, who was supposed to be Israel's defender, knew that without a brave champion, they might as well surrender.

So David went to Saul and said, "My King, do not lose heart! I will go and fight the giant. He doesn't look very smart!"

"I like your courage," King Saul said, "but you're only a small boy. He'll grab you, squish you, squash you, and then toss you like a toy!"

But David said, "God is my strength and nothing can compare with the power He once gave me to kill a lion and a bear!"

King Saul agreed, "Okay, kid, we'll put you in the fight.
I pray that God is with you and will help you win tonight."

"But just in case, you'll want to take my armor and my sword,
and fight with something more than just help from the Lord."

But in Saul's armor David felt like a sardine in a can.
He slipped it off and said, "Thanks, King, but I've got another plan."

"The Lord has always given me exactly what I need,
so with His help I'm absolutely sure that I'll succeed!"

Then David took his trusty staff and five stones from a stream, and armed with just a leather sling, he charged ahead full steam.

"I'll surely slay this big buffoon and do it with perfection! I know that I can win today for I have God's protection!"

Goliath took one look and said, "Why did you send a kid?
I challenged you to a he-man's fight, and you sent a little squid?!"

"You'd better run home, shepherd boy—I'll snap you like a twig!
Your sticks and stones can't break my bones. I'm just too strong and big!"

But David wasn't scared—he knew that God would be his guide.
He yelled, "I may be small, but I have God's strength on my side!"

"Today I'll strike you down and you'll not even lift your sword.
Today my God will beat you for this battle is the Lord's!"

Goliath and all the Philistines roared like the sound of thunder, and Goliath charged like a raging bull, which was his final blunder.

But David didn't flinch one bit and held his ground instead. He swung his sling and—WHACK!—he struck the giant on his head!

Goliath fell with a mighty THUD! and let out a final moan.
Goliath, the fearsome Philistine champ, was killed with a single stone!

All Israel cheered for David, shouting, "David is the man!"
The Philistines stopped their cheering, turned around, and ran, ran, ran!

King Saul and all the Israelites were feeling mighty fine,
so with David on their shoulders they marched across the battle line.

"Hip-hip-hooray! We won today! We think that David's great!
Hip-hip-hooray! We're here to stay! Let's go and celebrate!"

But David knew the reason for his victory that day,
and so he found a quiet place, alone, where he could pray.

He said, "I praise you, God, because I knew without a doubt
that You would give me super strength to knock Goliath out."

"Your love will never fail me.
You are with me even when
I face my greatest battles.
So, thank you, Lord. Amen."